SandCastle™

Primeros Sonidos

I0878869

Sara y Samuel

Cathy Camarena, M.Ed., and Gloria B. Ruff, M.Ed.

Consulting Editors

Lourdes Flores-Hanson, M.S.E., and Gloria Rosso-White

ABDO Publishing Company

capstone®

www.capstoneclassroom.com

Credits
Curriculum Coordinator: Nancy Tuminelly
Cover and Interior Design and Production: Mighty Media
Child Photography: Steven Wewerka, Wewerka Photography
Photo Credits: AbleStock, Brand X Pictures, Comstock, Stockbyte

ISBN 978-1-4966-0371-5 (paperback)

Printed in the United States of America.
042420 003442

SandCastle™ books are created by a professional team of educators, reading specialists, and content developers around five essential components that include phonemic awareness, phonics, vocabulary, text comprehension, and fluency. All books are written, reviewed, and leveled for guided and early intervention reading, and designed for use in shared, guided, and independent reading and writing activities to support a balanced approach to literacy instruction.

SandCastle Level: Beginning

Ss

ABCChDEFGH
IJKLLLMNÑOP
QRSTUVWXYZ

abcchdefgh
ijklllmnñop
qrstuvwxyz

Sara

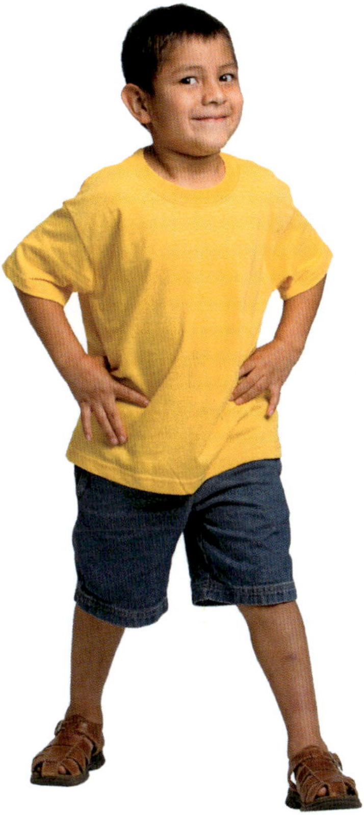

Samuel

sombrero

6

seis

sandía

sal

7

siete

Mira el .

El 6 es negro.

Mira la  .

La  es blanca.

El 7 es rojo.

Sara usa el sombrero.

El sombrero tiene una flor.

Samuel tiene una sandía.

A Samuel le gusta comer sandías.

La sandía es verde.

El sombrero está encima de la sandía.

¿Cuáles de estas cosas comienzan con **s**?

Más palabras que comienzan con s

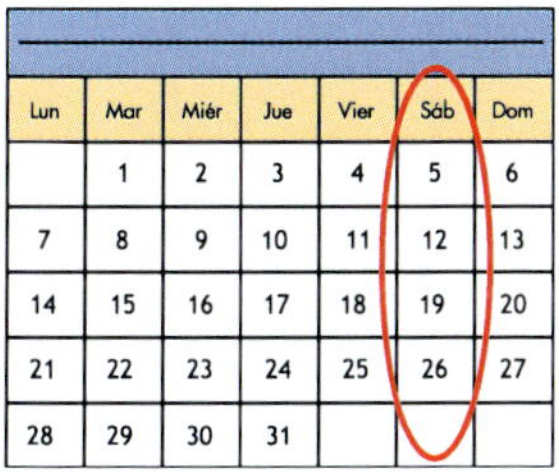

sábado

sacapuntas

sartén

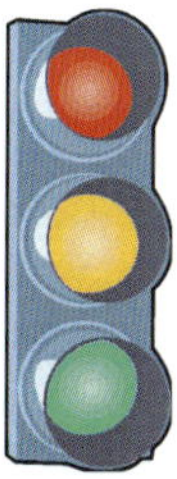

semáforo

silla

About SandCastle™

A professional team of educators, reading specialists, and content developers created the SandCastle™ series to support young readers as they develop reading skills and strategies and increase their general knowledge. The SandCastle™ series has four levels that correspond to early literacy development in young children. The levels are provided to help teachers and parents select the appropriate books for young readers.

Emerging Readers
(no flags)

Beginning Readers
(1 flag)

Transitional Readers
(2 flags)

Fluent Readers
(3 flags)

These levels are meant only as a guide. All levels are subject to change.

ABDO Publishing Company

www.abdopub.com

capstone

www.capstoneclassroom.com